THE BIG GAME

THE STANLEY CUP FINALS

HOCKEY'S GREATEST TOURNAMENT

Matt Scheff

SCORE BIG with sports fans, reluctant readers, and report writers!

Lerner™ Sports is a database profiling today's most popular sports stars! Introduce students to digital research skills through high-interest sports content, including soccer, hockey, football, baseball, basketball, and more. Hundreds of photos, thousands of bite-sized facts, and timely tie-ins to championship games make Lerner Sports the perfect bridge from the playing field to the library.

LERNER SPORTS FEATURES:
- Keyword search
- Topic navigation menus
- Fast facts
- Related bio suggestions to encourage more reading
- Admin view of reader statistics
- Fresh content updated regularly

and more!

Visit LernerSports.com for a free trial!

Lerner SPORTS

Copyright © 2021 by Lerner Publishing Group, Inc.

All rights reserved. International copyright secured. No part of this book may be reproduced, stored in a retrieval system, or transmitted in any form or by any means—electronic, mechanical, photocopying, recording, or otherwise—without the prior written permission of Lerner Publishing Group, Inc., except for the inclusion of brief quotations in an acknowledged review.

Lerner Publications Company
An imprint of Lerner Publishing Group, Inc.
241 First Avenue North
Minneapolis, MN 55401 USA

For reading levels and more information, look up this title at www.lernerbooks.com.

Main body text set in Conduit ITC Std.
Typeface provided by International Typeface Corp.

Designer: Viet Chu

Library of Congress Cataloging-in-Publication Data

The Cataloging-in-Publication Data for *The Stanley Cup Finals: Hockey's Greatest Tournament* is on file at the Library of Congress.
ISBN 978-1-5415-9758-7 (lib. bdg.)
ISBN 978-1-72841-420-1 (pbk.)
ISBN 978-1-72840-124-9 (eb pdf)

Manufactured in the United States of America
1-47862-48302-1/29/2020

Contents

Singing the Blues	4
Facts at a Glance	5
Chapter 1 Lord Stanley's Cup	6
Chapter 2 Memorable Moments	10
Chapter 3 Clutch Performers	18
Chapter 4 Stanley Cup Culture	24
THE CHAMPIONS	28
GLOSSARY	30
FURTHER INFORMATION	31
INDEX	32

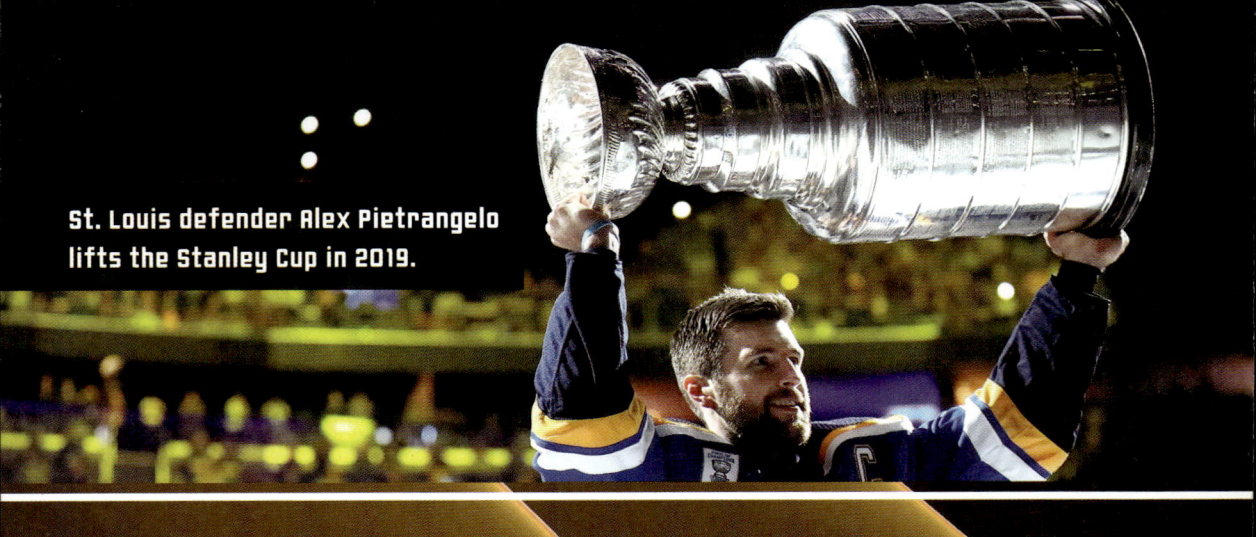

St. Louis defender Alex Pietrangelo lifts the Stanley Cup in 2019.

Singing the Blues

Game 2 of the 2019 Stanley Cup Finals started with a bang. The Boston Bruins and the St. Louis Blues each scored two goals in the first period. But defense dominated the next two periods, and neither team scored.

About four minutes into overtime, the Blues got their chance. A referee called a penalty on the Bruins. St. Louis peppered the goal with shots. Finally, Carl Gunnarsson scored with a hard slap shot. St. Louis players stormed the ice to celebrate the thrilling game-winner. The Blues went on to win their first Stanley Cup and claim the National Hockey League (NHL) championship.

Facts at a Glance

- The Stanley Cup existed long before the NHL did. Early on, any team—pro or amateur—could challenge for the cup.

- In 1975, the Buffalo Sabres won a Finals game played in dense fog. The fog was so thick that the opposing goaltender didn't see the game-winning shot in time to stop it.

- In 2018, the Vegas Golden Knights, in their first year of existence, made it to the Stanley Cup Finals.

- Players from the winning team can spend a day with the Stanley Cup. Players can take it almost anywhere—including on a roller coaster!

The 1914 Montreal Wanderers

CHAPTER 1
Lord Stanley's Cup

THE STANLEY CUP IS ONE OF THE MOST FAMOUS TROPHIES in sports. Canada's Frederick Arthur Stanley, Lord Stanley of Preston, wanted to honor the best hockey team in the land. In 1892, he bought the silver bowl-shaped trophy that became the symbol of the champions of Canadian hockey.

> Frederick Arthur Stanley was born in London, England, in 1841. In 1888, he became governor general of Canada.

Early on, any successful team could challenge the team that held the Stanley Cup. In 1908, the Montreal Wanderers defended the cup five times. Two years later, officials agreed to award the Stanley Cup to one team each season. The NHL formed in 1917. In the 1926–1927 season, the Cup formally became the NHL's championship trophy.

The Growing League

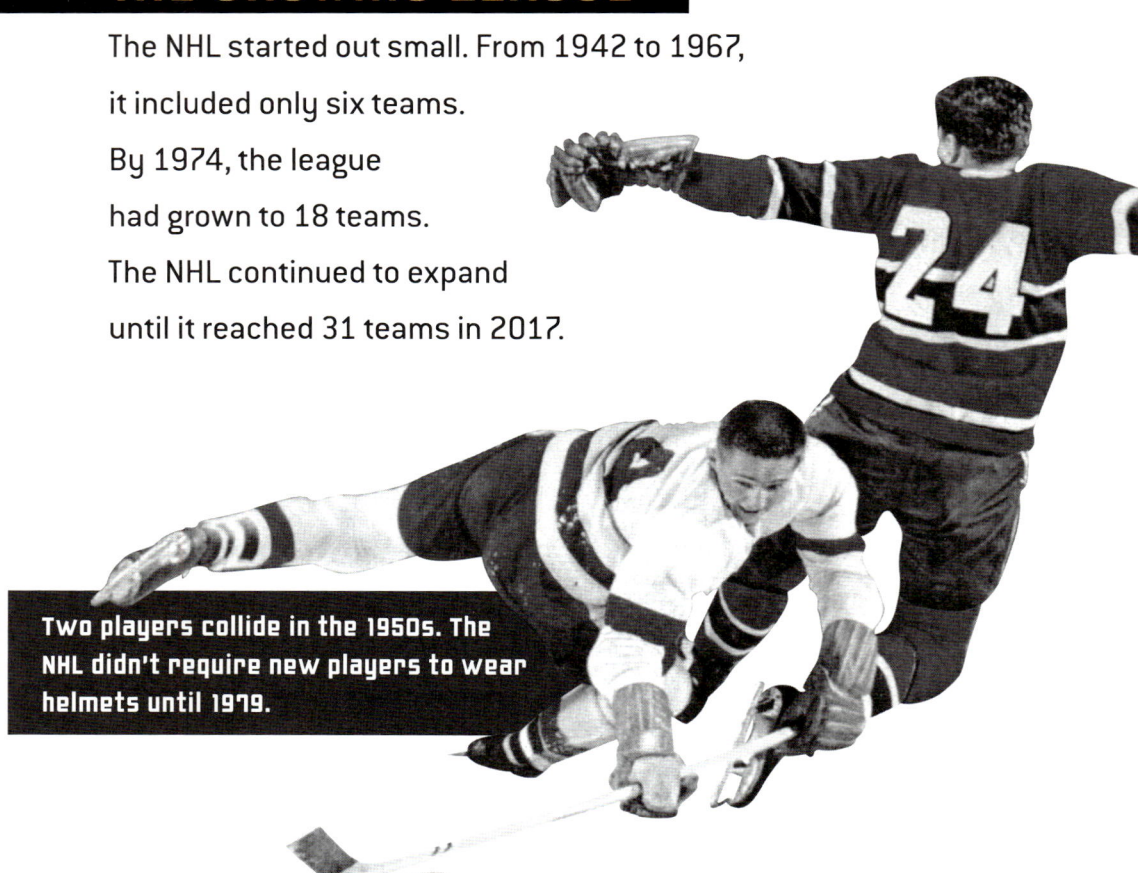

The NHL started out small. From 1942 to 1967, it included only six teams. By 1974, the league had grown to 18 teams. The NHL continued to expand until it reached 31 teams in 2017.

Two players collide in the 1950s. The NHL didn't require new players to wear helmets until 1979.

Inside the Game

Professional hockey isn't just for men. In 2015, the National Women's Hockey League formed. The league's championship trophy, the Isobel Cup, is named for Isobel Gathorne-Hardy, Lord Stanley's daughter. The Boston Pride won the first Isobel Cup. In 2019, the Minnesota Whitecaps won the Cup in their first season in the league!

As the league grew, so did the excitement of the Stanley Cup Finals. Stars such as Maurice "Rocket" Richard, Wayne Gretzky, and Sidney Crosby ignited fan interest in hockey's biggest event. In 2019, 8.2 million fans tuned in to watch the Blues beat the Bruins in the winner-take-all Game 7.

Alexander Steen of the Blues looks for a teammate to pass the puck to during the 2019 Stanley Cup Finals.

Goalie Bernie Parent watches the puck through the fog.

CHAPTER 2

Memorable Moments

THE STANLEY CUP FINALS HAVE GIVEN FANS MANY weird, wild, and wonderful memories. One of the weirdest came in 1975, when the Philadelphia Flyers faced the Buffalo Sabres in Game 3. In the first period, officials stopped the game because a bat was swooping down over the ice.

Then the game got weirder. It was a warm, humid day in Buffalo. Soon a blanket of fog covered the ice. The game ended in overtime when Buffalo's Rene Robert shot the puck past Philadelphia goalie Bernie Parent. The fog was so thick that Parent saw the shot too late to stop it. The fog helped Buffalo win the game, but the Flyers got the last laugh when they won the series.

In 524 career NHL games, Rene Robert scored 222 goals.

Inside the Game

In the 1942 Finals, the Detroit Red Wings charged out to a 3–0 series lead. They were one win from a championship. But the Toronto Maple Leafs won the next four games to complete the biggest comeback in Finals history.

Orr's Flying Goal

One of the most famous goals in Stanley Cup history came off the stick of Boston Bruins defenseman Bobby Orr in 1970. Boston hadn't won the Cup in 29 years. Fans were hungry for a victory.

Orr (*center*) reacts to his game-winning goal.

Bruins players celebrate Orr's goal.

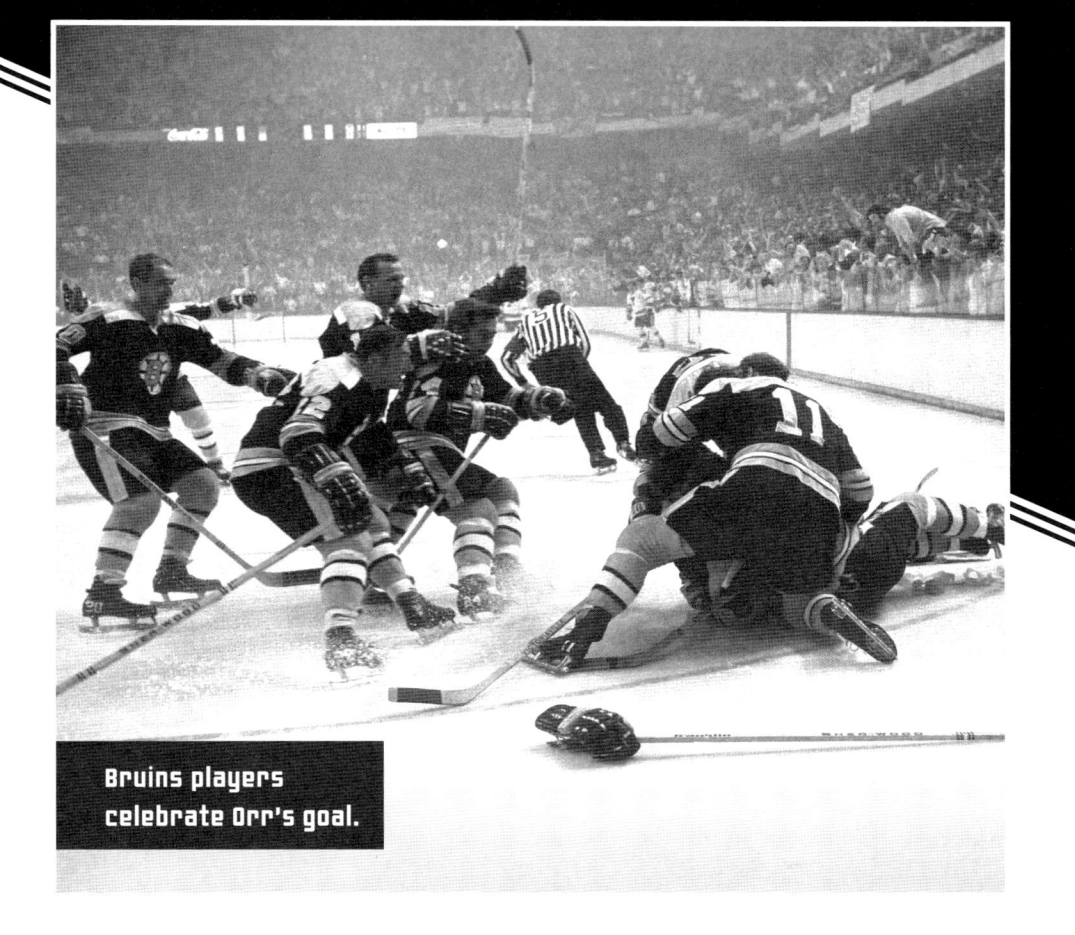

Game 4 went to overtime tied 3–3. Orr zipped a pass to teammate Derek Sanderson. Orr raced toward the net as Sanderson slid the puck in front of the goal. Desperate, a St. Louis defender tripped Orr. But it was too late. Orr flew through the air as the puck went into the net. The Flying Goal clinched the cup for Boston, and the long wait was over.

Now You See It, and Now You Don't

In 2010, Chicago Blackhawks star Patrick Kane scored one of the greatest—and most confusing—goals in Stanley Cup history. In overtime of Game 6 against the Flyers, Kane skated toward the Philadelphia net. He flicked a shot on goal from deep in the corner. The puck flew toward the goalie and slid away, and the teams began to charge in the other direction.

Kane (*in white*) skates with the puck in Game 6. He scored 10 goals during the 2010 playoffs.

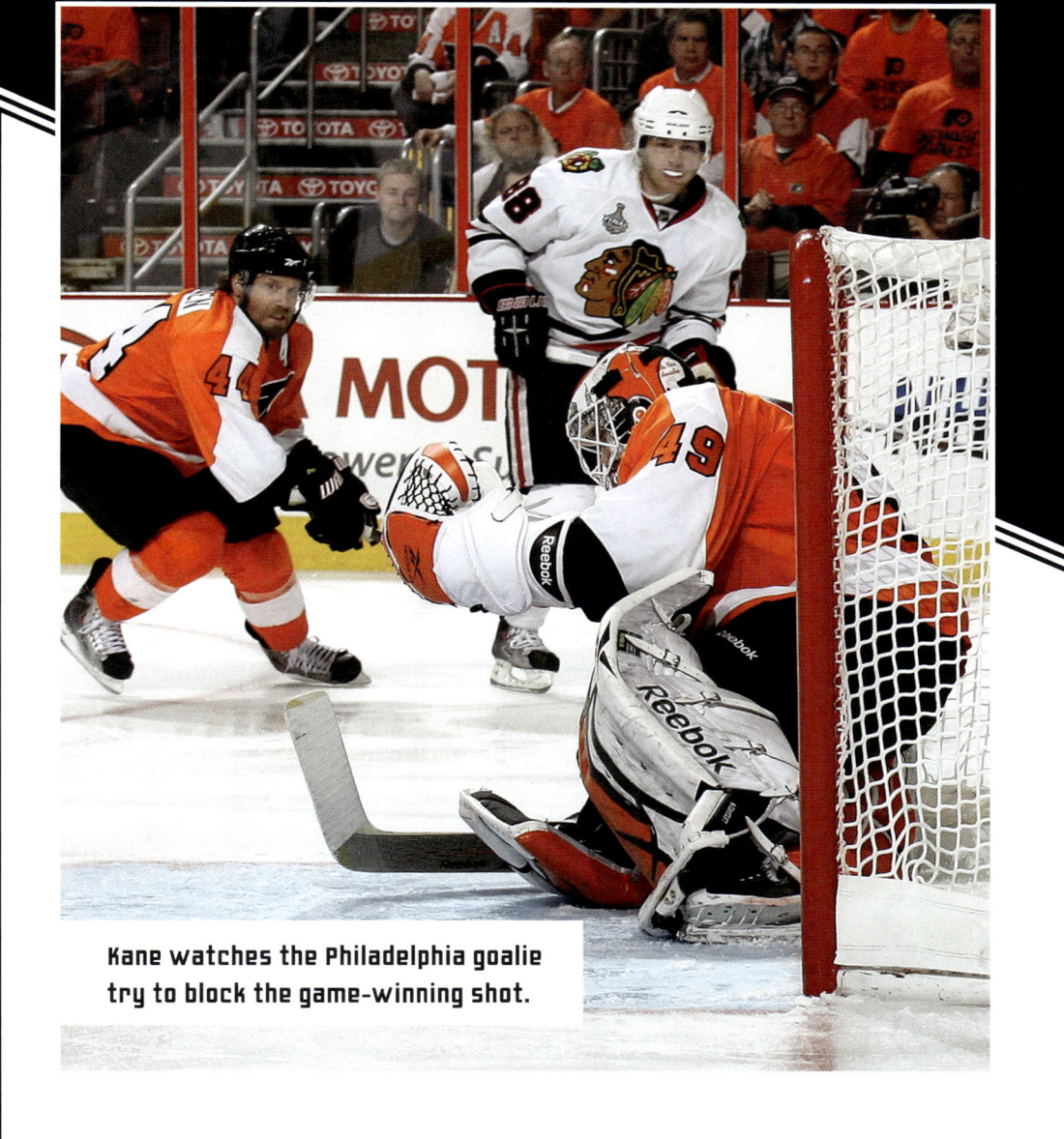

Kane watches the Philadelphia goalie try to block the game-winning shot.

Then officials stopped play. The referee signaled that Kane had scored a goal. The game—and the series—was over. Replay showed that Kane's shot had gone into the goal for a fraction of a second. It was a historic goal, and almost nobody noticed it!

Welcome to the NHL

In the 2017–2018 season, the Vegas Golden Knights joined the NHL as an expansion team. The Golden Knights were built largely from NHL castoffs—players other teams didn't think were worth keeping. No one expected much of the team in its first season.

But the Golden Knights shocked the sports world. They made the playoffs. Then they advanced all the way to the Stanley Cup Finals! Vegas won Game 1 before superstar Alex Ovechkin and the Washington Capitals ended their amazing run. But many fans will never forget the expansion team that nearly won it all.

Golden Knights forward Jonathan Marchessault skates past a defender during the 2018 playoffs.

William Carrier of the Golden Knights chases the puck during Game 5 of the 2018 Stanley Cup Finals.

17

Three defenders try to stop Wayne Gretzky (*center*) during a game in 1984. Many fans consider Gretzky to be the best player in NHL history.

CHAPTER 3
CLUTCH PERFORMERS

THE NHL'S STARS SHINE BRIGHTEST IN THE STANLEY Cup Finals. The body checks are harder, the defense is tougher, and the goals are more exciting. Sometimes, one player's clutch performance can be the difference between victory and defeat. The greatest performers helped their teams win it all on hockey's biggest stage.

18

ROCKET RICHARD

Rocket Richard was one of the NHL's first true superstars. From 1944 to 1960, the high-scoring forward led the Montreal Canadiens to 13 Finals, winning eight of them. He gave his greatest playoff performance in 1944. In nine playoff games, he scored 12 goals!

Henri Richard

Rocket Richard is more famous than his younger brother Henri. But no player in NHL history has won more Stanley Cups than Henri Richard. The 5 feet 7 inch (1.7 m) forward was nicknamed the Pocket Rocket. He was part of the greatest dynasty the NHL has ever seen. Richard and the Canadiens won the Cup 11 times from 1956 to 1973.

Wayne Gretzky

Fans call Wayne Gretzky the Great One. He entered the NHL in 1979 with the Edmonton Oilers and went on to rewrite the league's record books. He was a brilliant passer and a deadly goal scorer. He won four Stanley Cups and racked up 382 points in 208 NHL playoff games.

Mark Messier

Wayne Gretzky was Edmonton's biggest star during the team's dynasty in the 1980s. But many fans think Mark Messier was their most important player for his toughness and leadership. He won four Stanley Cups alongside Gretzky. Then Messier added a fifth championship with the Oilers after Gretzky left the team. Messier won a sixth title with the New York Rangers in 1994.

Patrick Roy

No goaltender was more clutch in the playoffs than Patrick Roy was. He won Stanley Cups with the Canadiens in 1986 and 1993. Then he won two more with the Colorado Avalanche in 1996 and 2001. The athletic goalie won 151 playoff games, an NHL record.

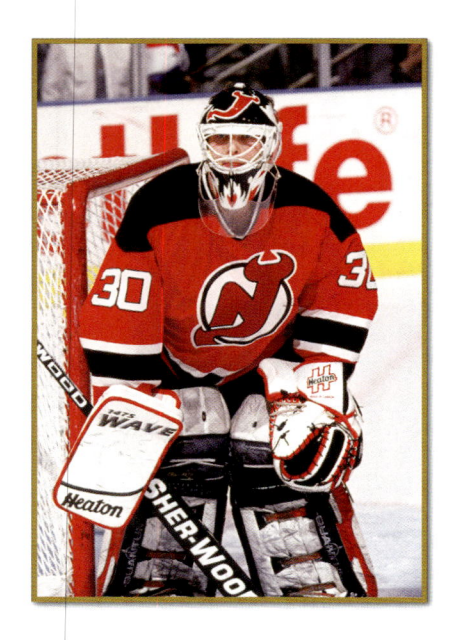

Martin Brodeur

Goaltender Martin Brodeur played with an old-school style. Like many goalies of earlier eras, he rarely dropped to his knees to block the puck. Brodeur and the New Jersey Devils went to the Finals five times from 1995 to 2012. They won the title three times. Brodeur won 113 playoff games, the second most of all time.

Alex Ovechkin

Few players have had the incredible scoring ability of Alex Ovechkin. The Washington Capitals forward has won the league goal-scoring title a record eight times. In 2018, the Capitals won their first Stanley Cup. Ovechkin had 5 points in the five-game series.

SIDNEY CROSBY

Sidney Crosby was just 22 years old when he led the Pittsburgh Penguins to the Stanley Cup title in 2009. Sid the Kid wasn't always the highest-scoring player on the ice. But his leadership and ability to control the puck helped the Penguins win three Stanley Cups.

Blues fans cheer for their team.

CHAPTER 4

Stanley Cup Culture

NOTHING CAN MATCH THE THRILL OF THE STANLEY CUP Finals. Every face-off, pass, and save matters. The goal is the Stanley Cup, and fans love the excitement. On game night, fans pack into sold-out arenas wearing their team's colors. The excitement grows as famous singers perform the national anthems of the United States and Canada. By the time the puck drops, the noise in the arena is deafening.

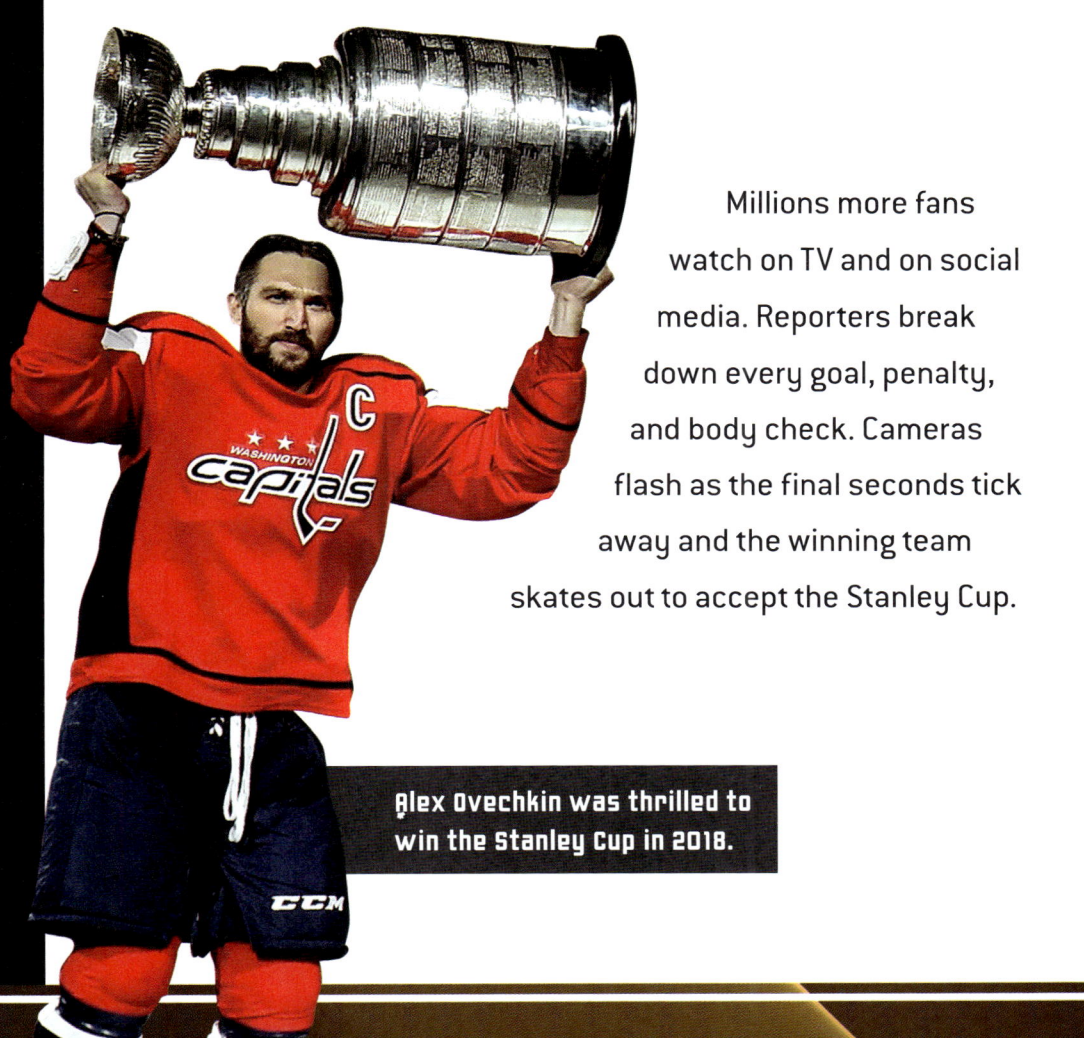

Millions more fans watch on TV and on social media. Reporters break down every goal, penalty, and body check. Cameras flash as the final seconds tick away and the winning team skates out to accept the Stanley Cup.

Alex Ovechkin was thrilled to win the Stanley Cup in 2018.

Inside the Game

In Game 1 of the 1990 Finals, the Oilers and Bruins played three overtime periods. Edmonton won the game more than 55 minutes into overtime. But that game doesn't compare to the 1936 semifinal between the Detroit Red Wings and Montreal Maroons. That game was scoreless for six overtimes before Detroit finally won!

The Tour

When the series ends, the fun is just beginning. The winning team has 100 days to take the Stanley Cup on tour. Usually, each player and coach gets a day with the trophy. They bring it to their hometowns, colleges, or somewhere fun.

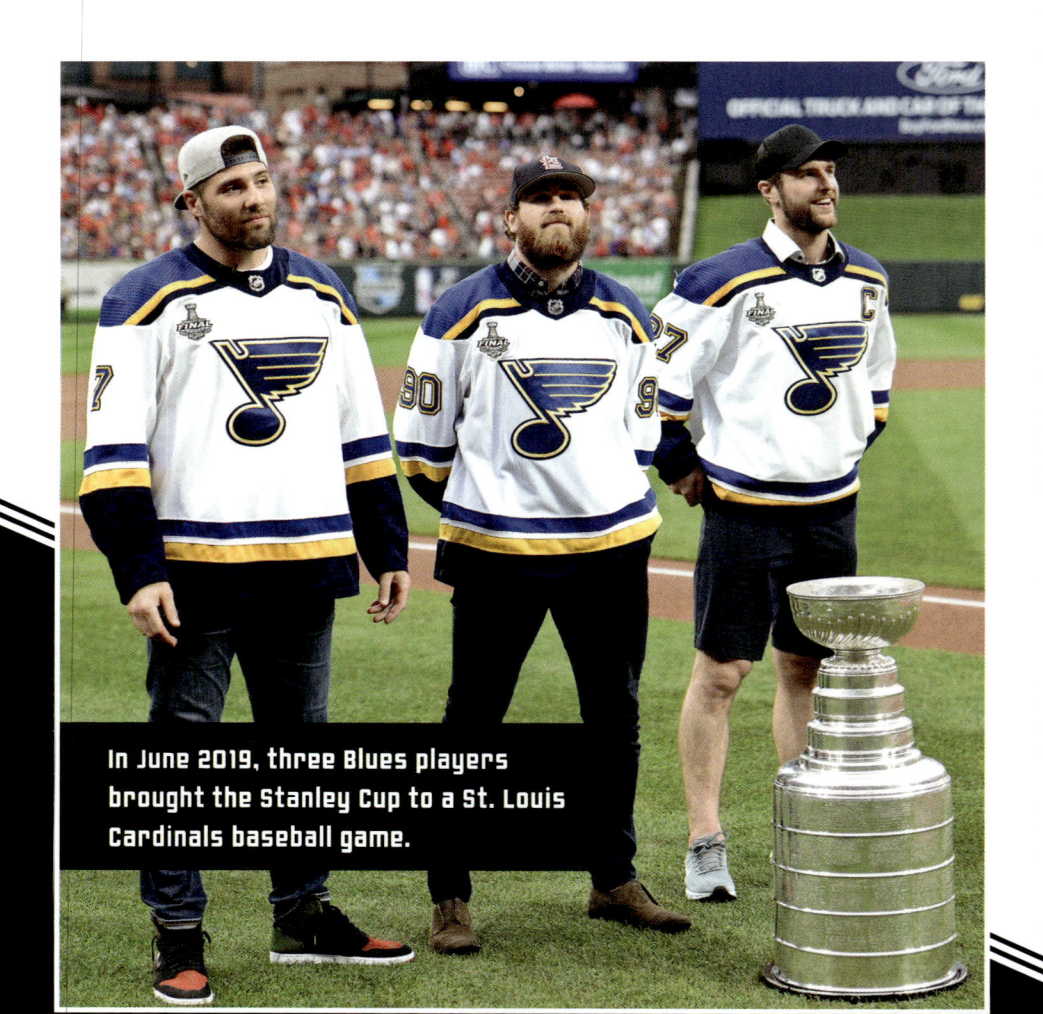

In June 2019, three Blues players brought the Stanley Cup to a St. Louis Cardinals baseball game.

In 2012, Willie Mitchell of the Los Angeles Kings brought the Stanley Cup to Canada's Mount St. Benedict.

One player brought the Stanley Cup on a roller coaster ride. Another took it out for a round of golf. The trophy even took a lap at Indianapolis Motor Speedway with race car driver Mario Andretti. Nothing is off-limits, as long as it doesn't damage the famous trophy. After 100 days, the players and coaches get back to work. The NHL season is about to start. The chase for Lord Stanley's Cup begins again.

THE CHAMPIONS

Year	Champion
2019	St. Louis Blues
2018	Washington Capitals
2017	Pittsburgh Penguins
2016	Pittsburgh Penguins
2015	Chicago Blackhawks
2014	Los Angeles Kings
2013	Chicago Blackhawks
2012	Los Angeles Kings
2011	Boston Bruins
2010	Chicago Blackhawks
2009	Pittsburgh Penguins
2008	Detroit Red Wings
2007	Anaheim Ducks
2006	Carolina Hurricanes
2005	No Stanley Cup Finals due to labor dispute
2004	Tampa Bay Lightning
2003	New Jersey Devils
2002	Detroit Red Wings
2001	Colorado Avalanche
2000	New Jersey Devils
1999	Dallas Stars
1998	Detroit Red Wings
1997	Detroit Red Wings
1996	Colorado Avalanche
1995	New Jersey Devils
1994	New York Rangers
1993	Montreal Canadiens

Year	Champion
1992	Pittsburgh Penguins
1991	Pittsburgh Penguins
1990	Edmonton Oilers
1989	Calgary Flames
1988	Edmonton Oilers
1987	Edmonton Oilers
1986	Montreal Canadiens
1985	Edmonton Oilers
1984	Edmonton Oilers
1983	New York Islanders
1982	New York Islanders
1981	New York Islanders
1980	New York Islanders
1979	Montreal Canadiens
1978	Montreal Canadiens
1977	Montreal Canadiens
1976	Montreal Canadiens
1975	Philadelphia Flyers
1974	Philadelphia Flyers
1973	Montreal Canadiens
1972	Boston Bruins
1971	Montreal Canadiens
1970	Boston Bruins
1969	Montreal Canadiens
1968	Montreal Canadiens
1967	Toronto Maple Leafs
1966	Montreal Canadiens
1965	Montreal Canadiens

Year	Champion	Year	Champion
1964	Toronto Maple Leafs	1945	Toronto Maple Leafs
1963	Toronto Maple Leafs	1944	Montreal Canadiens
1962	Toronto Maple Leafs	1943	Detroit Red Wings
1961	Chicago Black Hawks	1942	Toronto Maple Leafs
1960	Montreal Canadiens	1941	Boston Bruins
1959	Montreal Canadiens	1940	New York Rangers
1958	Montreal Canadiens	1939	Boston Bruins
1957	Montreal Canadiens	1938	Chicago Black Hawks
1956	Montreal Canadiens	1937	Detroit Red Wings
1955	Detroit Red Wings	1936	Detroit Red Wings
1954	Detroit Red Wings	1935	Montreal Maroons
1953	Montreal Canadiens	1934	Chicago Black Hawks
1952	Detroit Red Wings	1933	New York Rangers
1951	Toronto Maple Leafs	1932	Toronto Maple Leafs
1950	Detroit Red Wings	1931	Montreal Canadiens
1949	Toronto Maple Leafs	1930	Montreal Canadiens
1948	Toronto Maple Leafs	1929	Boston Bruins
1947	Toronto Maple Leafs	1928	New York Rangers
1946	Montreal Canadiens	1927	Ottawa Senators

Glossary

body check: a blocking of an opposing player with the body

clutch: having the ability to perform in high-pressure situations

dynasty: a team that enjoys long-term success with multiple championships

expansion team: a team added to an existing league

forward: a player who plays at the front of a team's formation near the opponent's goal

overtime: a 20-minute period added to the end of a game when the score is tied

penalty: punishment for breaking a rule

point: a stat that represents a goal and an assist combined

referee: an official who enforces a game's rules

slap shot: a shot made with a swinging stroke

Further Information

Fishman, Jon M. *Hockey's G.O.A.T.: Wayne Gretzky, Sidney Crosby, and More*. Minneapolis: Lerner Publications, 2020.

Hewson, Anthony K. *Alex Ovechkin*. Minneapolis: Lerner Publications, 2020.

Hockey Hall of Fame
https://www.hhof.com/

Morey, Allan. *The Stanley Cup Finals*. Minneapolis: Bellwether Media, 2019.

National Hockey League
http://nhl.com

Sports Illustrated Kids—Hockey
https://www.sikids.com/hockey

Index

Buffalo Sabres, 5, 10–11

Canada, 6–7, 24

Crosby, Sidney, 9, 23

Gretzky, Wayne, 9, 20–21

Montreal Canadiens, 19

National Women's Hockey League, 8

Orr, Bobby, 12–13

Ovechkin, Alex, 16, 22

record, 20, 22

Richard, Maurice "Rocket," 9, 19–20

Stanley, Frederick Arthur, 6

Stanley Cup tour, 26

St. Louis Blues, 4, 9

Vegas Golden Knights, 5, 16

Washington Capitals, 16, 22

Photo Acknowledgments

Image credits: Dilip Vishwanat/Getty Images, p. 4; sdominick/Getty Images, p. 5; Bruce Bennett Studios/Getty Images, pp. 6, 8, 10, 12, 20 (top), 20 (bottom); Universal History Archive/Getty Images, p. 7; Steve Babineau/NHLI/Getty Images, pp. 11, 21 (top); Bettmann/Getty Images, pp. 13, 19; Bill Smith/NHLI/Getty Images, p. 14; Len Redkoles/NHLI/Getty Images, p. 15; Lachlan Cunningham/Getty Images, p. 16; Jeff Bottari/NHLI/Getty Images, p. 17; Focus On Sport/Getty Images, p. 18; Graig Abel/Getty Images, p. 21 (bottom); John Giamundo/Getty Images, p. 22 (top); McDermott/NHLI/Getty Images, p. 22 (bottom); Dave Reginek/NHLI/Getty Images, p. 23; Dave Sandford/NHLI/Getty Images, p. 24; Patrick McDermott/NHLI/Getty Images, p. 25; Rick Ulreich/Icon Sportswire/Getty Images, p. 26; Jeff Vinnick/NHLI/Getty Images, p. 27. Design elements: Tuomas Lehtinen/Getty Images; zhengshun tang/Getty Images. Cover image: Bruce Bennett/Getty Images.